Moses and the Gr
from the *Read Wit*

CANDLE
BOOKS

Pharaoh's Daughter Finds Moses

Exodus 2

An Israelite woman gave birth to a son. But Pharaoh had ordered all Hebrew baby boys to be killed. She placed him in a basket and hid it among the reeds near the River Nile.
The baby's sister, Miriam, stood at a distance to see what would happen to him.

Pharaoh's daughter went down
to the Nile to take a bath.
She saw the basket among the reeds
and sent her slave girl to get it.
She opened the basket and saw the baby.
He was crying, and she felt sorry for him.
"This is one of the Hebrew babies," she said.

So she took the baby and Miriam's mother nursed him. When the child grew older, she took him to Pharaoh's daughter. He became her son, and she named him Moses.

Moses and the Burning Bush
Exodus 3–4

One day Moses was watching sheep in the desert. Moses saw a bush that was on fire, but it didn't burn up.

God called to Moses from within the bush, "Moses! Moses!"
And Moses said, "Here I am."
"Don't come any closer," God said.
"Take off your sandals.
You are standing on holy ground."

Then God said, "I have seen the misery
of my people in Egypt. I have heard them crying.
I know they are suffering.
I have come down to rescue them. So now, go.
Tell Pharaoh to let my people go."
So Moses took his wife and sons and
started back to Egypt.

The First Five Plagues
Exodus 5–9

Moses and his brother Aaron went to Pharaoh and said, "Let my people go so they can worship God in the desert or he may send plagues." Pharaoh said, "I don't know your God. And I will not let your people go."

So God struck the water of the Nile,
and it turned into blood.
The fish in the Nile died.
The river smelled so bad that
the Egyptians could not drink the water.
But Pharaoh would not let the people go.

Then Moses said to Pharaoh, "Let my people go." Pharaoh said, "No!" So God sent frogs to cover the land. The frogs came into the palace and jumped on the beds.

They came into the kitchens and filled the ovens. Pharaoh said to Moses, "Pray to your God to take these frogs away, and I will let your people go." Moses did. The frogs died.
But Pharaoh would not let the people go.

Then Moses said to Pharaoh,
"Let my people go." And Pharaoh said, "No!"
So God turned the dust of Egypt into gnats.
There were gnats on all the people
and on every animal. But Pharaoh was stubborn
and would not let the people go.

So God sent swarms of flies.
The flies covered the people and the ground.
They poured into the palace.
Pharaoh called to Moses, "Pray to your God to take these flies away.
Then I will let your people go."
Moses did. The flies disappeared.
But Pharaoh would not let the people go.

Then Moses said, "Let my people go."
Pharaoh said, "No!"
So God sent a terrible plague on all the animals.
The horses, the donkeys, the camels,
the sheep and the goats all died.
But Pharaoh would not let the people go.

Four More Plagues
Exodus 9–12

Moses tossed some ashes into the air.
God turned the ashes into a fine dust
that made sores break out
on all the people and the animals.
But Pharaoh did nothing.

So God sent thunder and hail.
Hail beat down everything growing in the fields.
It stripped every tree.
Pharaoh said to Moses, "I've been wrong.
You are right. Pray to your God to stop
the thunder and hail."
Moses did. The thunder and hail stopped.
But Pharaoh would not let the people go.

So God sent swarms of locusts.
They covered the ground until it was black.
They ate all that was left after the hail.
Nothing green was left. Pharaoh said to Moses,
"Pray to your God to take these locusts away.
Then I will let your people go."
Moses did. The locusts flew away.
But Pharaoh would not let the people go.

Then Moses pointed to the sky.
Darkness covered Egypt for three days.
No one could see anyone else.
Pharaoh called Moses, "Go, worship your God.
But leave your flocks and herds behind."
Moses said, "Our animals must go with us."
So Pharaoh would not let the people go.
God said to Moses, "I will send one more plague.
After that, Pharaoh will let you go."

The Last Plague
Exodus 12

Moses said to the elders of Israel, "Each man is to take a lamb for his family. The animal must be one year old.

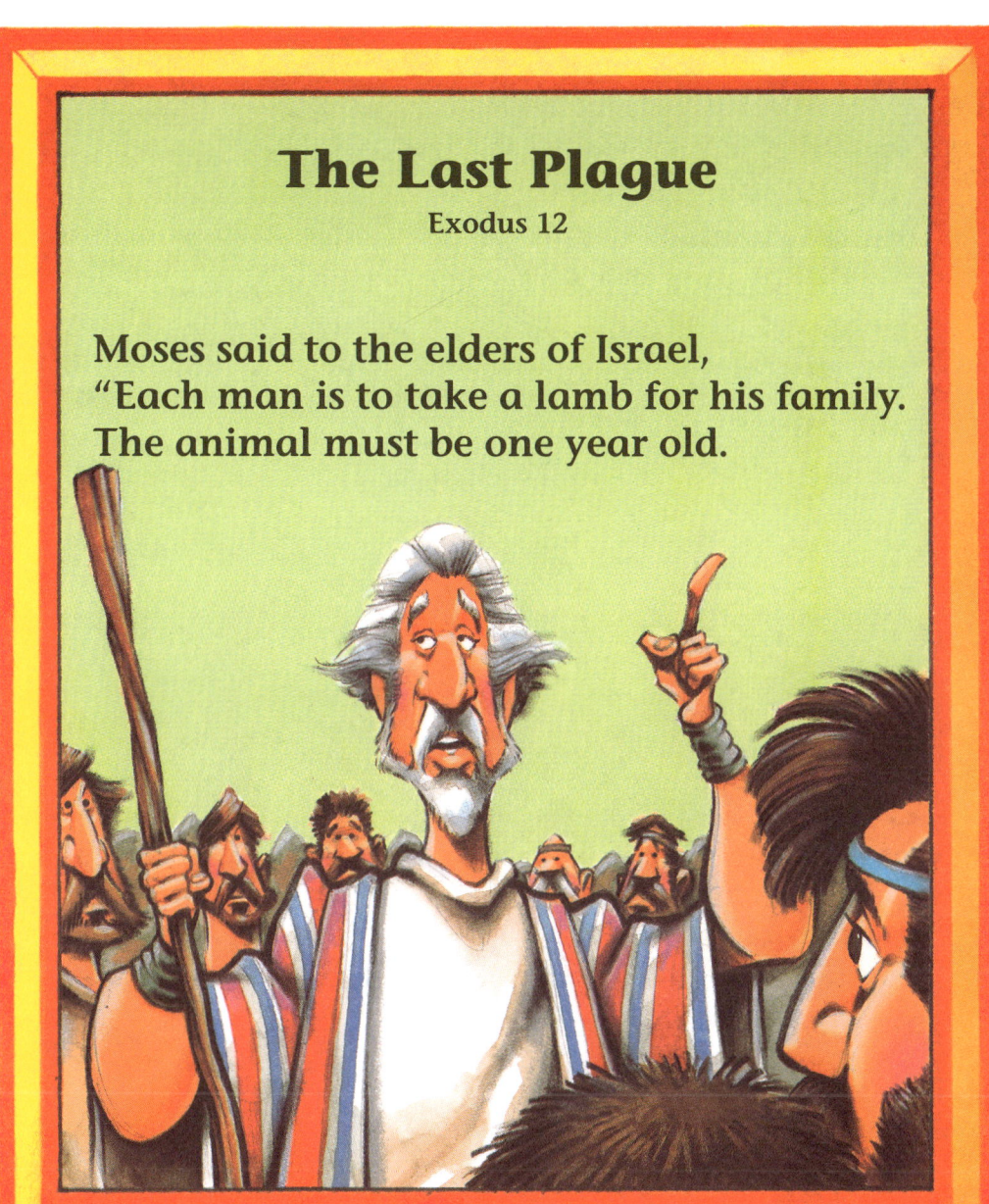

Kill the lambs at sunset.
Put some of the blood on the top and
on both sides of the door of your house.
When God goes through the land
to strike down the Egyptians, he will see
the blood and will pass over that doorway.
He will not let the destroyer enter
your houses and strike you down."
The Israelites did just what God said.

At midnight God struck down all the firstborn.
There was loud wailing in Egypt, for there
was not a house without someone dead.
Pharaoh called Moses and said,
"Up! Leave my people.
Take your flocks and herds, and go."

The Israelites Leave Egypt
Exodus 12–13

So the Israelites left Egypt.
There were about 600,000 men,
besides women and children.
The Egyptians urged the people to hurry.
"Otherwise," they said, "we will all die!"
By day God went ahead of the Israelites in a pillar
of cloud and by night in a pillar of fire.
So the Israelites could travel by day or night.

Crossing the Red Sea
Exodus 14

When Pharaoh was told that the Israelites had fled, he changed his mind and said, "What have I done?" So the Egyptians—all Pharaoh's horses and chariots, horsemen and troops— chased the Israelites.

As Pharaoh approached, the Israelites looked up, and there were the Egyptians!
They were terribly afraid.
They said to Moses, "What have you done? It would have been better for us to serve the Egyptians than to die in the desert!"
Moses answered the people, "Don't be afraid. God will fight for you."

The Israelites went through the sea on dry ground, with a wall of water on their right and on their left.

All Pharaoh's horses and chariots
followed them into the sea.
Moses stretched out his hand,
and the sea went back to its place.
The water covered the entire
Egyptian army.
Not one of them survived.
That day God saved Israel
from the Egyptians.
The people put their trust in God.

Moses and the Great Escape

Illustrated by Dennis Jones
Edited by Doris Rikkers and Jean E. Syswerda

READ WITH ME BIBLE
Copyright © 1993 by the Zondervan Corporation

Scripture portions adapted from The Holy Bible,
New International Version
Copyright © 1973, 1978, 1984 by International Bible Society

The 'NIV' and 'New International Version' trademarks are registered in the United States Patent and Trademark Office by International Bible Society.

All rights reserved. No part of this publication may be reproduced, stored in a retrieval system, or transmitted in any form or by any means – electronic, mechanical, photocopy, recording or any other – except for brief quotations in printed reviews, without the prior permission of the publisher.

ISBN 1 85985 193 2
Published in the UK by Candle Books 1998
Distributed by STL
PO Box 300, Carlisle,
CA3 0QS

Worldwide coedition organised and produced by Angus Hudson Ltd, Concorde House, Grenville Place, Mill Hill, London NW7 3SA, England
Tel: +44 181 959 3668
Fax: +44 181 959 3678

Printed in England